I broke a bone for the first time in my life—the middle finger of my right hand. I couldn't even hold a pen, which meant I was a manga artist who couldn't draw manga. So it was a serious event in its own way. The nail had received a heavy blow and was torn off, and the doctor scared me by saying it might not grow back again. Eventually, I could remove the cast, but it was still too painful to bend the finger. I thought it was the end of my career as a manga artist. But somehow I managed to recover, and we were able to release this new volume. Ahhh...I'm so glad.

— Koji Inada

Author Riku Sanjo and artist Koji Inada were both born in Tokyo in 1964. Sanjo began his career writing a radio-controlled car manga for the comic **Bonbon**. Inada debuted with **Kussotare Daze!!** in **Weekly Shonen Jump**. Sanjo and Inada first worked together on the highly successful **Dragon Quest–Dai's Big Adventure**. **Beet the Vandel Buster**, their latest collaboration, debuted in **Monthly Shonen Jump** in 2002 and was an immediate hit, inspiring an action-packed video game and an animated series on Japanese TV.

BEET THE VANDEL BUSTER
VOL. 11
The SHONEN JUMP Manga Edition

STORY BY RIKU SANJO
ART BY KOJI INADA

Translation/Naomi Kokubo
Touch-Up & Lettering/Mark McMurray
Design/Andrea Rice
Editor/Shaenon K. Garrity

Managing Editor/Frances E. Wall
Editorial Director/Elizabeth Kawasaki
VP & Editor in Chief/Yumi Hoashi
Sr. Director of Acquisitions/Rika Inouye
Sr. VP of Marketing/Liza Coppola
Exec. VP of Sales & Marketing/John Easum
Publisher/Hyoe Narita

Printed in the U.S.A.

Published by VIZ Media, LLC
P.O. Box 77064
San Francisco, CA 94107

SHONEN JUMP Manga Edition
10 9 8 7 6 5 4 3 2 1
First printing, April 2007

viz
media

www.viz.com

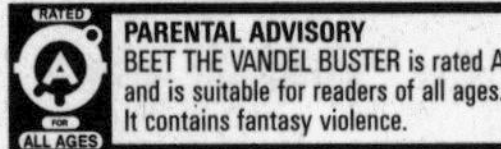
RATED
A
FOR
ALL AGES
PARENTAL ADVISORY
BEET THE VANDEL BUSTER is rated A
and is suitable for readers of all ages.
It contains fantasy violence.

THE WORLD'S
MOST POPULAR MANGA
SHONEN
JUMP
www.shonenjump.com

SHONEN JUMP Manga Edition

Beet™
THE VANDEL BUSTER

Volume 11

Story by **Riku Sanjo**

Art by **Koji Inada**

KISSU

An old friend of Beet's, he is a genius and a master of the Divine Attack. He's trying to redeem himself after working for Vandels.

BEET

The hero of this story. Believing in justice, he sets out on a journey to save the world. He received five Saiga weapons from the Zenon Warriors.

MILFA

Milfa is one of the Broad Busters, an elite class of high-level Busters. She has an extremely upbeat personality and is a huge fan of the Zenon Warriors.

POALA

Beet's childhood friend has an unyielding spirit. She joins Beet as the second of the Beet Warriors and sets out on the journey with him. She is skilled at Kenjutsu, the art of the samurai sword, as well as the Divine Attack.

SLADE

Although he acts cold and rude, he cares about Beet and has a friendly rivalry with him as a Buster.

STORY

CHARACTERS

CRUSS

One of the Zenon Warriors. He has lost his memory and now lives quietly as an artist.

BELTORZE

Known as the "King of Tragedy," he is a seven-star Vandel widely feared by humans.

GARONEWT

A resourceful Vandel with impregnable defenses. He's widely hated by other Vandels.

SHAGIE

The "world's busiest Vandel," he is in charge of evaluating and supervising all Vandels. He is the Chief of the Dark House of Sorcery.

"Vandels"...In this story, that's what we call evil creatures with magical powers. One day they appeared on the surface of the Earth, releasing monsters and destroying whole nations. People called this seemingly endless era "The Dark Age." Beet, a young boy who believes in justice, binds himself to a contract and becomes a Vandel Buster. Early in his career, Beet stumbles into a battle between the Zenon Warriors and a Vandel named Beltorze, where he suffers a fatal injury. He miraculously survives by receiving the Saiga of the Zenon Warriors. Carrying on the Zenon Warriors' dream of peace, Beet sets out with his friends on a quest to destroy all Vandels.

In Bekatrute, Beet finds one of the Zenon Warriors, Cruss, who has lost his memory. When Cruss is kidnapped by Garonewt, the Beet Warriors travel to Maniyon Island to rescue him. After a desperate battle, Garonewt unleashes his true fighting power and uses underhanded tactics, taking Cruss as a human shield. Beet strikes back at Garonewt with all his might...

Beet
THE VANDEL BUSTER

11

Chapter 39: The Immovable Giant Falls!

!
VOOM

THE GRAVITY...
...LIFTED!

Y...

Y...
YOU...

YOU WHELP!
BA DOOM
BOOM

!?

SHAAA
BOOOOOM

SHUK
VOOOOOM

SHAA

ANOTHER STRIKE!
YOU CAN DO IT!
RIGHT, BLADE?

SHING

GRP
ALL RIGHT !!
BAM

CLANK
CLUNK

DAK

SHK

SHIKKK

READ THIS WAY

ZENON...
...WINZARD!

RIP

RRRIP

BOOOOM

READ THIS WAY

VMMMM
SHA...

VMMM
SHOOF

SHF

TAKKA

YOU DID IT...
... POALA!

YUP!

BUT...

HE DISAPPEARED!

WAS HE BLOWN TO PIECES?
OR...

CHECK IT OUT.

!

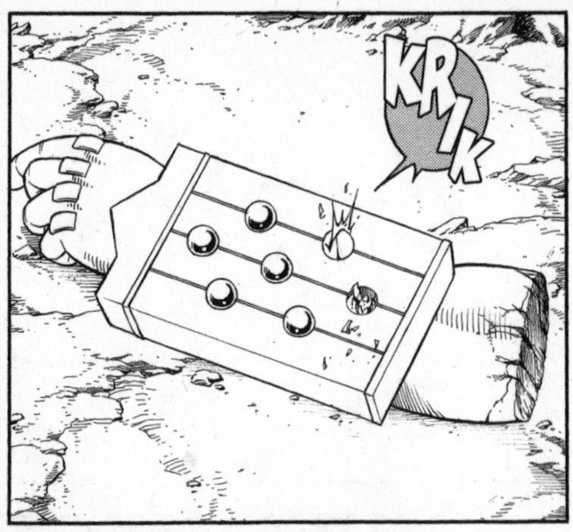
KRIK

COME TO THINK OF IT...RIGHT BEFORE GRINEED DIED, HIS STARS DID THE SAME THING...

EVEN IF A VANDEL'S ARM IS SEVERED, THE STARS DON'T BREAK.
IT'S ONLY WHEN A VANDEL DIES THAT THE STARS ***CRACK***...

KRIK KRIK KRAK

NO DOUBT ABOUT IT.
HE'S...

ARRGH...

HEY!
WHAT ABOUT CRUSS? HE WAS HELD BY THAT HAND!

IT LOOKS LIKE GARONEWT NEEDED BOTH HANDS TO MAINTAIN THE GRAVI-ZONE.
THAT'S WHY THE EFFECT VANISHED WHEN HIS ARM WAS SEVERED...
WOBBLE

WHEN THAT HAPPENED, I RAN UP TO SAVE MR. CRUSS...
...BUT I GUESS WE GOT HIT IN A BAD SPOT...

WHAT?
CRUSS!
DAKKA

READ THIS WAY

!?

NO... HE'S OKAY...
GUYS...
WAAAH
THE ONE WHO GOT HIT WAS...

...ME!
WHOOMP

THROB
THROB
THROB

OH, *DEAR* ...

...
HE'S EITHER A SUPERMAN OR A TOTAL AMATEUR.
GEEZ.

HE MAY NOT LOOK IT, BUT HE'S PRETTY AMAZING...
...CRUSS!

MAYBE WE SHOULD'VE LET YOU JOIN US, EH?

NOT AS GOOD AS YOU GUYS WERE, THOUGH!
HA HA

IT'S A FINE TEAM.
YES.
I CAN SEE THAT.

YOU TURNED OUT TO BE A LONG-ANTICIPATED NEW WEAPON, AFTER ALL!

OF COURSE!

TOOK YOU LONG ENOUGH TO...

A LONG-ANTICIPATED NEW WEAPON!!
SHING
OKAY!!
LET ME JOIN YOU!
I'LL JOIN THE ZENON WARRIORS NOW!!!
SHK

CR...
CRUSS?

SNIFF

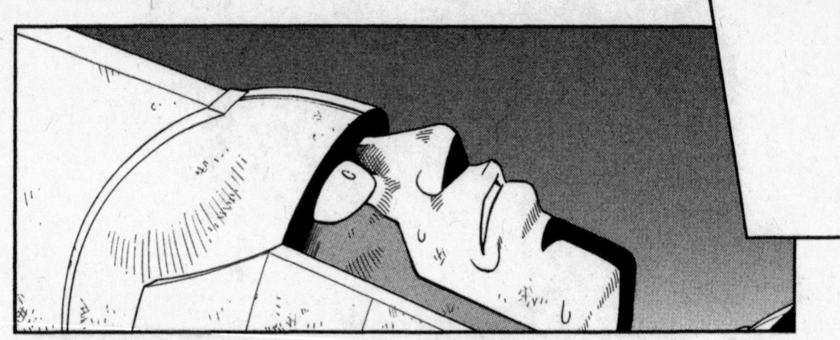

WH-
WHERE
AM I?
DID
SOME-
ONE
RESCUE
ME?
HELLO?

READ THIS WAY

!

RO...
RODINA!

WELCOME TO MY ROOM...
...GARO-NEWT.

WHAT'S GOING ON?
WHY DID YOU SAVE ME?

SAVE YOU?
NOT AT ALL!

I JUST THOUGHT I'D VISIT YOUR DEATHBED. I WANTED TO *THANK* YOU.
KRRRK

YOU'RE FATALLY INJURED.
THERE'S NO HOPE FOR YOU NOW.

!!

AS I'D HOPED, YOU TORMENTED BEET AND THE OTHERS...
...FORCING THEM TO PUSH THEIR POWERS TO THEIR LIMIT.
AND THEN...
...WHEN YOU'D ALMOST WON, YOU DUG YOUR OWN GRAVE WITH YOUR SILLY *PLAYFULNESS*.

IT WAS LOVELY.
YOU WERE THE PERFECT ONE TO GO FIRST.
I'M GLAD I CHOSE YOU.
...?

THUD

WHAT'RE YOU TALKING ABOUT?

I BECAME THE FIRST FIGHTER BY...

BY CHEATING YOUR WAY IN?

YOU STILL THINK SO?

HEH.

YOU THINK NO ONE KNOWS ABOUT YOUR TRICK CARDS, AND HOW THEY RESPOND TO YOUR DARK POWER?

ARGH

WHY DON'T YOU TAKE A CLOSER LOOK AT THE CARDS YOU'VE GOT HIDDEN IN YOUR ARM?

CLANK
SHOOF
TUK
TUK

SHOOOF

TUK
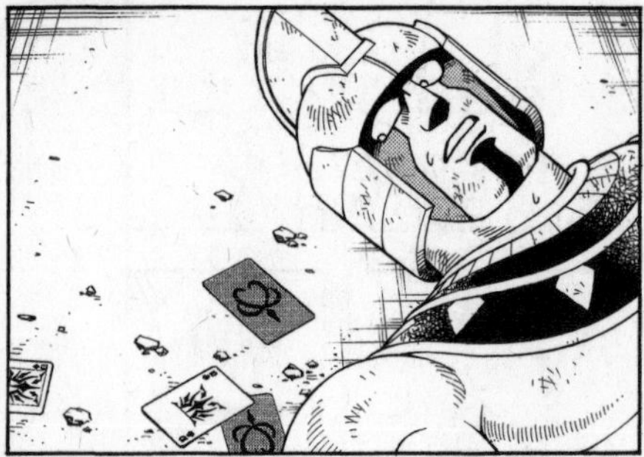

THAT'S RIGHT.
THOSE CARDS ARE *MINE*.

TH... THAT'S A LIE!
WHEN DID YOU ...

AND WHY?
WHY WOULD SHE CHOOSE TO GO *LAST*?

SHOOOM

READ THIS WAY

UGH!
KRRRK
KRRRK

POOR GARONEWT. DIMWITTED, SELF-ABSORBED AND UTTERLY *CLUELESS*. YOU ACTUALLY THINK YOU'RE A *TACTICIAN*!
YOU TRIED TO USE US AS YOUR *PAWNS*!

BUT I USED *YOU* AS *MY* PAWN...
...IN THIS GAME.
KRRK
UGH...
ARRRGH!
KRRRRK
KRRRK

YOU MUST BE TIRED.
REST WELL.

AH!!

TMP

SHUU

THE NEXT ONE IS BARON, THE KING OF THE SKY.
TIK
HE'S TOO POWERFUL FOR THEM TO BEAT WITH SHEER LUCK.

I WONDER WHAT...
...THE BEET WARRIORS WILL DO.
OH, YES...

TEE HEE
...AND THAT LOVELY BOY...

GRM GRM
GRM GRM
GRM GRM

TAK

HEE HEE
HEE

SHOOF

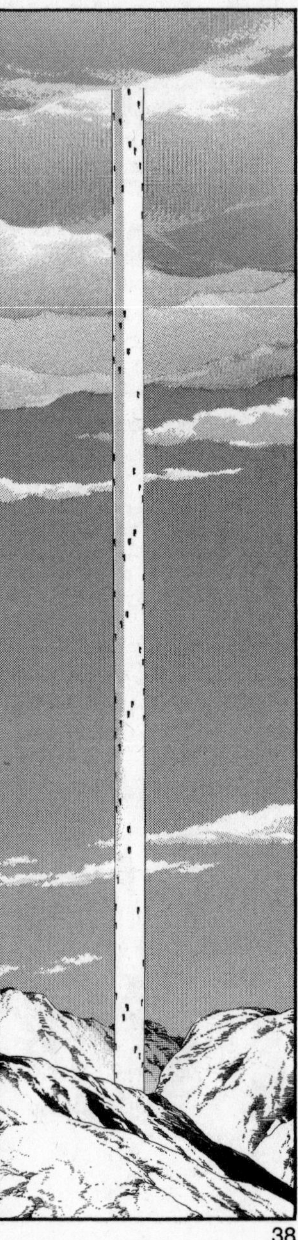

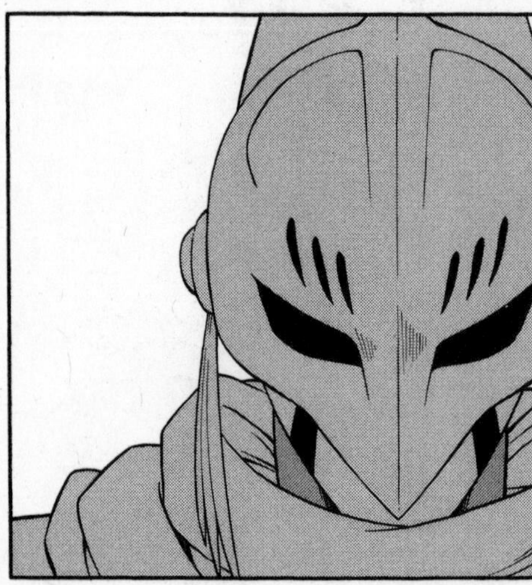

READ THIS WAY

...

IT'S UNUSUAL TO RECEIVE GUESTS HERE.

SHF...

I HEAR GARO'S DEAD.
OH HO...
YOU KNOW...
...WHAT THAT MEANS.
SHF...

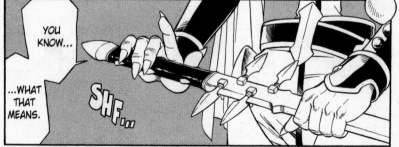

READ THIS WAY

IF YOU DIE, IT'S *MY* TURN.

WELL, SIR?

ISN'T THAT RIGHT ?

HEH

SHING...

BEET
THE VANDEL BUSTER

Chapter 40: The Memory of That Day

FWAP

TAK

THAT MEANS ...
SNAP

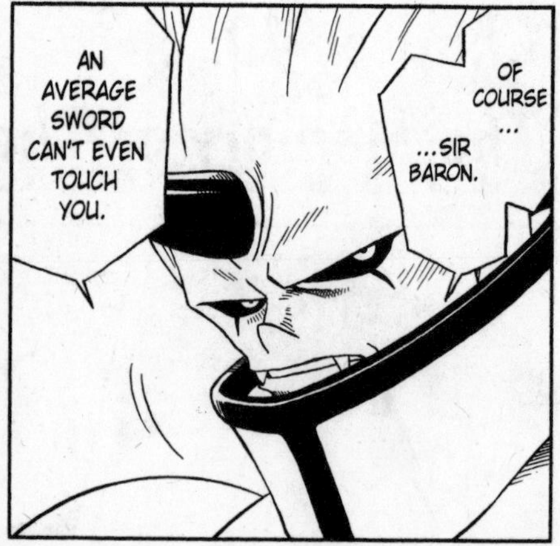
AN AVERAGE SWORD CAN'T EVEN TOUCH YOU.
OF COURSE ...
...SIR BARON.

READ
THIS
WAY

...I NEED TO USE *THIS!*
SHOOF...

TWAANG

FANG STYLE TRANSMIGRATION!
YOUR FAMOUS SECRET TECHNIQUE.

...

SO YOU'RE SERIOUS, HYSTARIO.

I ADVISE AGAINST IT.
I'D GO EASY ON AN OPPONENT WHOSE POWER WAS SIGNIFICANTLY INFERIOR TO MINE.

BUT WITH SOMEONE ON ***YOUR*** LEVEL, I WON'T HOLD BACK!

TWAANG
SHF

GRRM
RRRRM
RRM

!!!!

GRP

KNOCK IT OFF.

NOA, THE VANDEL SCHOLAR!

WHERE'D THIS GUY COME FROM?
IT'S NOT SUPER-SPEED OR ANYTHING LIKE THAT...

URRK...
...

SHF

IT WAS A JOKE.
JUST A JOKE.
I DID IT TO CHEER SIR BARON ON.

Y'KNOW ...
...MAYBE A PACIFIST LIKE YOU IS THE *REAL* STRONGEST VANDEL.

WHO KNOWS ...
...PRO-FESSOR ?

...

HEH
HEH...
SOME CHEER, EH?

YOU GOT ME OUT OF A POINTLESS FIGHT...
FWSH
...NOA.

I HAVE NO INTEREST IN FIGHTING VANDELS.

YOU'RE ONLY INTERESTED IN FIGHTING STRONG HUMANS.
FROM WHAT I HEAR, YOU EVEN LET THE PROMISING ONES GET AWAY, HOPING TO COME BACK WHEN THEY'RE STRONGER.
I KNOW ...
...SIR.

I BELIEVE THAT'S WHAT ANNOYS HYSTARIO.

READ
THIS
WAY

WITH GARONEWT, HE KNEW THE FIGHT WOULD BE SETTLED QUICKLY. BUT WITH YOU, IT COULD BE DRAGGED OUT FOREVER.

GARO-NEWT?
WHAT A FOOL. HE WAS ALMOST IN-DESTRUCTIBLE, BUT THAT SHORT FUSE OF HIS...

I CAME BECAUSE I, TOO, WANTED TO KNOW YOUR INTENTIONS.

WHAT ARE YOU GOING TO DO...
...ABOUT BEET?

I'LL FIGHT HIM.
FIGHTING HUMANS IS WHAT MAKES US VANDELS.

I'M FAITHFUL TO MY INSTINCTS.

YOUR PEACEFUL LIFE...
...MUST BE PURE PAIN...
...NOA.

PERHAPS...
...BUT I DISLIKE FIGHTING, SIR.

IS THAT SO?

LET ME MEDITATE AGAIN.

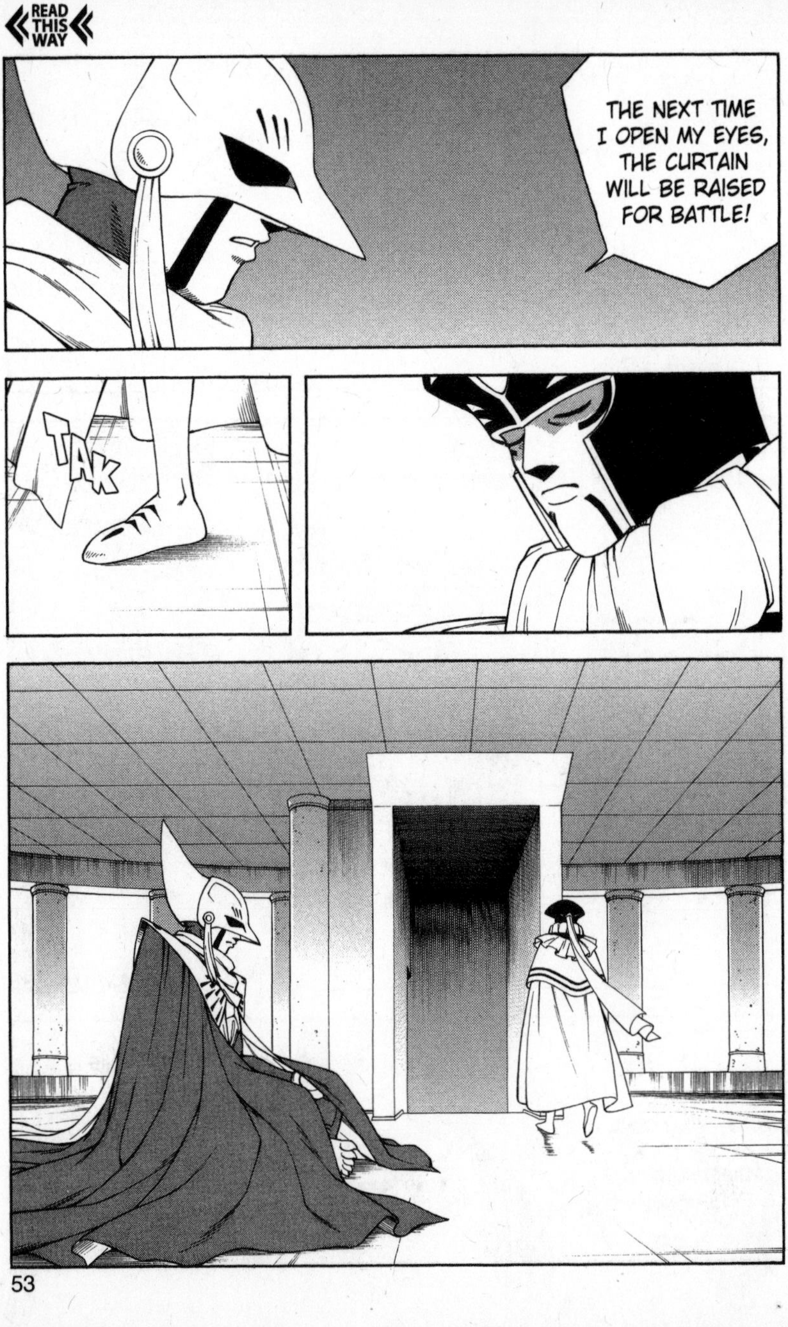

READ THIS WAY

THE NEXT TIME I OPEN MY EYES, THE CURTAIN WILL BE RAISED FOR BATTLE!

TAK

WHOA!
"TEMPORARY LEVEL CERTIFICATE"!
I'VE NEVER *SEEN* THIS BEFORE.
IS THIS FOR REAL?

THIS IS A SPECIAL TREATMENT BECAUSE YOU'RE WITH MILFA, THE BB.
YOUR BRANDING AND REWARD MONEY WILL COME *AFTER* YOUR PUNISHMENT IS DETERMINED.

READ THIS WAY

UNLESS I DO THIS, I CAN'T PAY SLADE FOR FIGHTING ALONG WITH YOU.

IT...IT'S KIND OF NICE.
BECAUSE OF ME, WE COULDN'T RAISE OUR LEVELS FOR SO LONG. WE STILL DON'T GET ANY **MONEY**, BUT...

I'M ALREADY LEVEL 27!
ME!

HMPH
I GUESS WE **DID** DEFEAT GRINEED AND GARONEWT...

THUMP

LOOKS LIKE I'M RICH.

THIS BUSTER GROUP SURE GETS ME INTO...
...SOME WILD STUFF.

HEY, SLADE.
CHECK IT OUT. ☆

I'M NOW LEVEL 43!
NOT *BAD*, HUH? ♡
TEE HEE

READ THIS WAY

YEAH, YEAH.
I KNOW YOU'RE HOT, LADY.
SHUF

HMPH!
YOU'RE NO FUN TO TEASE, SLADE!
BORING!

WHAT'S BEET UP TO?
BAH
I THINK HE WENT TO HAVE A TALK WITH DARLING CRUSS.

IS THAT RIGHT...

UM...
"DARLING"
?

WOOM
SHING
SHIK
THUK

WUPP
VOOM

THUKKA
GRP
VWSH
EEEE
BAM
HRE
S
GRRP

READ THIS WAY

HE LEARNS EVERYTHING YOU TEACH HIM, LIKE SAND SUCKING UP WATER.

WHAT A BOY.
TUP

YES.

IT'S LIKE A DREAM!
I'M SO GLAD...
...I CAN LEARN THIS STUFF RIGHT FROM YOU, CRUSS!

OOPS.
NOT CRUSS, HUH?

CA...
WHAT WAS IT AGAIN?

YOU CAN CALL HIM CRUSS NOW.

CRUSS...
...NOW THAT YOU'RE BACK TO NORMAL...

READ THIS WAY

VMMMMM

GRP

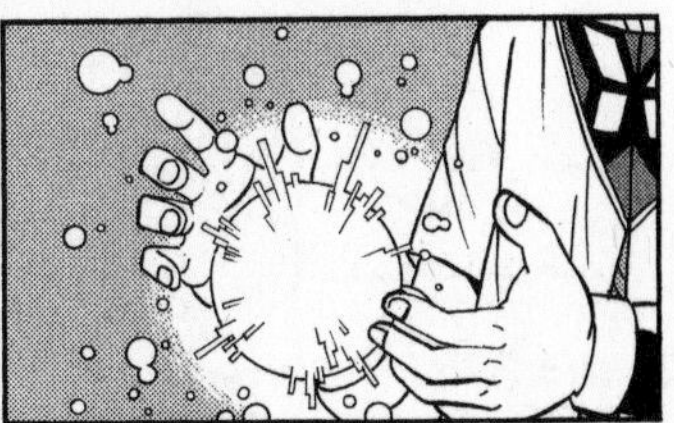

SHF

...

GRRR

IT'S NO GOOD.
BUT YOU GOT YOUR MEMORY BACK!

SHF

THAT DAY ...
...WHEN WE FOUGHT BELTORZE...
...ALL FIVE OF US PUSHED OUR SAIGAS, WITH OUR LIFE FORCES INSIDE THEM, INTO YOUR BODY.
SHAAAA
DOOOM

IT WAS LIKE SACRIFICING BODY AND SOUL.
WE EXCHANGED OUR ULTIMATE WEAPONS, POLISHED IN BATTLE, FOR THE ENERGY OF LIFE.

SUCH LOSS IS UNFATHOMABLE.
IT ISN'T SOMETHING ONE CAN GET BACK SO EASILY.

I SEE...

MY LIFE COST YOU SO MUCH, AND I'M STILL USING WHAT YOU GAVE ME.

IT ALL FEELS SO *HEAVY*...

BUT AT THE TIME, I NEVER DREAMED YOU'D BE ABLE TO MATERIALIZE THE FIVE SAIGAS!

GO AHEAD AND KEEP USING THE SHIELD AS YOUR OWN.

NOW THAT YOU'RE CLOSE TO MASTERING THE EXCELLION BLADE ITSELF...

YOU MEAN MY OWN SAIGA?

...I DON'T THINK IT'LL BE TOO LONG BEFORE YOU AWAKEN YOUR OWN POWER.
!?

NO WAY!
I'M STILL STRUGGLING TO MASTER WHAT YOU GUYS GAVE ME...

NO, WHAT YOU'RE DOING IS MUCH HARDER. MASTERING THOSE FIVE SAIGA IS TOUGHER THAN GIVING BIRTH TO A NEW ONE.
YOU MIGHT EVEN BE ABLE TO REACH THE NEXT STEP, A STEP WE CAN'T IMAGINE...

...JUST LIKE HE DID ON THAT DAY!

"HE"?
YOU MEAN ZENON?

READ THIS WAY

YEAH!
TELL ME, CRUSS!
THAT DAY, AFTER I PASSED OUT...
...YOU ALL FACED DOWN BELTORZE!

SO?
WHAT REALLY HAPPENED?

...

COME TO THINK OF IT, I FOUND YOU MORTALLY WOUNDED ON A BEACH HERE...
...BUT THE BATTLE TOOK PLACE ON THE OTHER SIDE OF THE OCEAN, DIDN'T IT?

WHY...
...WERE YOU HERE?

THAT DAY...
...THE TRUE BATTLE BETWEEN THE ZENON WARRIORS AND BELTORZE, THE KING OF TRAGEDY...

...TOOK PLACE AFTER YOU PASSED OUT, BEET.

ARRRGH!!

BSSH
DOOM
CRUSS !!

UGH!
PLIP
HE ATTACKED WITH DARK POWER!
NO WAY!
WE'RE ON OUR LAST LEGS...
...BUT HE'S *GOT* TO BE OUT OF DARK POWER BY NOW!

GRRRRM
RRRRM

GRRRRM

HEY!

HE'S A FIVE-STAR VANDEL, ISN'T HE?

WHY'RE THERE ONLY FOUR?

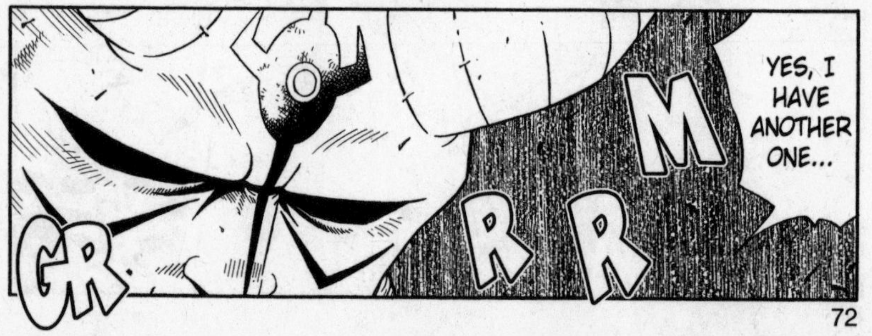
YES, I HAVE ANOTHER ONE...
GRRRM

SHK

NOW...

...I'LL SHOW YOU ALL FIVE!

SHK SHHK

SHING

OOOOM

D

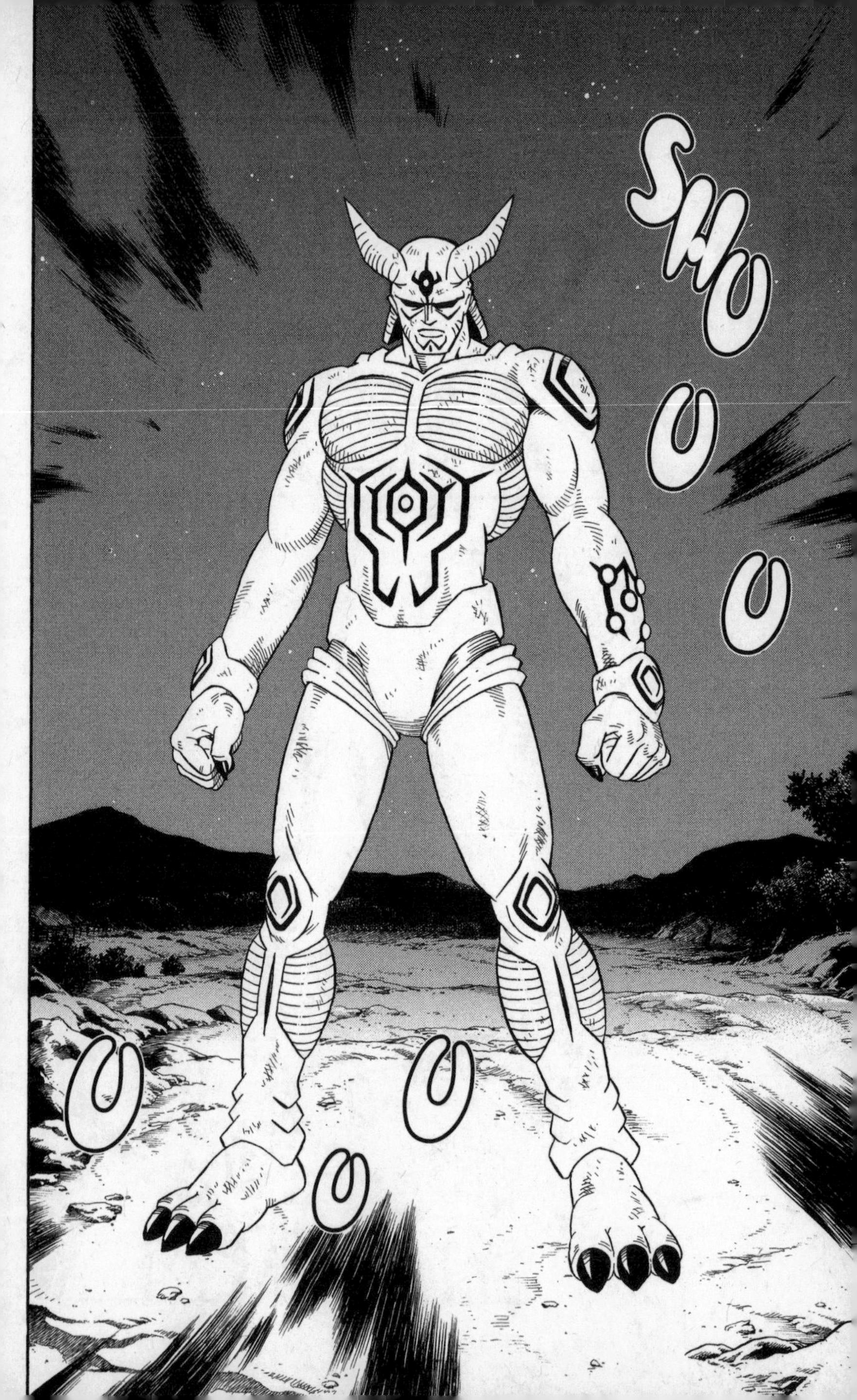
SHUUUUUU

READ THIS WAY

FWOOM

NO...
BZZT
BZZT
IT CAN'T BE!
BZZZT

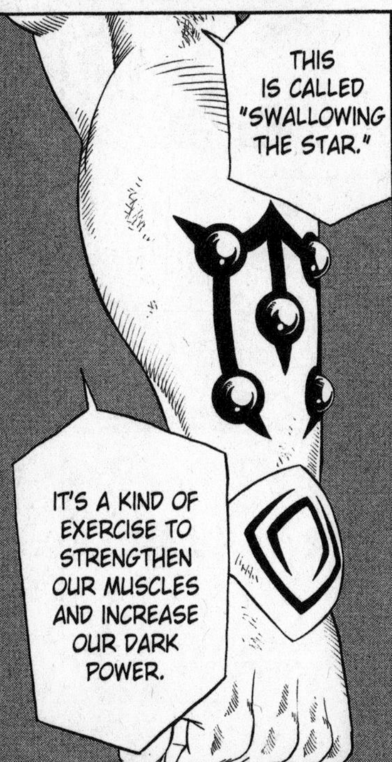
THIS IS CALLED "SWALLOWING THE STAR."
IT'S A KIND OF EXERCISE TO STRENGTHEN OUR MUSCLES AND INCREASE OUR DARK POWER.

EVERY VANDEL IS BORN WITH ONE STAR. BY SEALING DARK POWER INSIDE THE FIRST STAR AND KEEPING IT INSIDE THE BODY...
...A VANDEL CAN LEARN TO GET BY ON LIMITED DARK POWER!

IMPOSSIBLE...
IF THAT'S THE CASE...

DOES THAT MEAN HE WASN'T FIGHTING AT FULL POWER UNTIL NOW?

I JUST HAVE AN EXTRA LEVEL YOU DIDN'T KNOW ABOUT, THAT'S ALL.

READ
THIS
WAY

DON'T FEEL TOO BAD.
I STILL RESPECT YOU FOR FIGHTING ME THIS FAR.

BUT IT'S AN ACCIDENTAL VICTORY.

I'M JUST LUCKY THAT I HAPPENED TO PRACTICE THIS TECHNIQUE.

RRRRR
RM
LET ME GIVE YOU YOUR REWARD!

READ THIS WAY

HEH ...
HEH HEH HEH ...
DOESN'T LOOK GOOD, GUYS.

WE'VE GOT NOTHING LEFT...

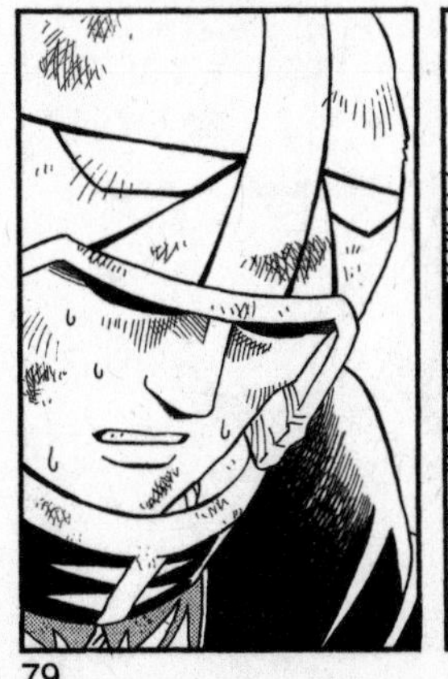

DON'T GIVE UP...
...LAIO.
...?!

WHAT DO I ALWAYS SAY?
YOUR ONLY WEAKNESS IS THAT YOU GIVE UP TOO SOON.

HEH...
THE LAST LECTURE I'LL EVER GET FROM YOU.

MAYBE.
GRRP
IF THAT'S SO...

READ THIS WAY

...YOU'D BETTER REMEMBER...
...WHAT I'M ABOUT TO DO!

WAAA

Chapter 41: Zenon Shines!!

SHF
BAH
WOOSH
HEY, ZENON!
WHAT ARE YOU THINKING?

OOSH
WH
RRM
R
R

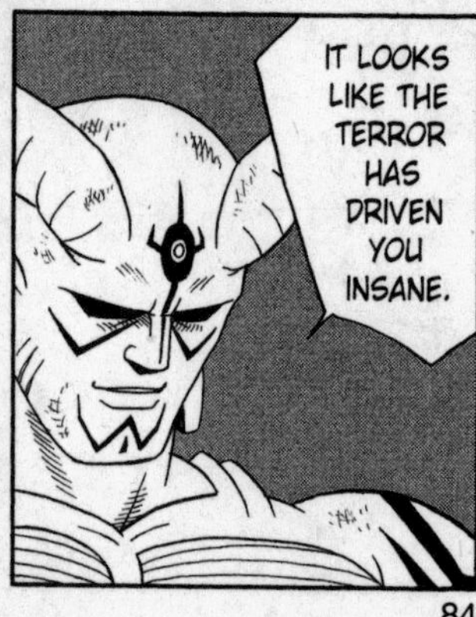
IT LOOKS LIKE THE TERROR HAS DRIVEN YOU INSANE.

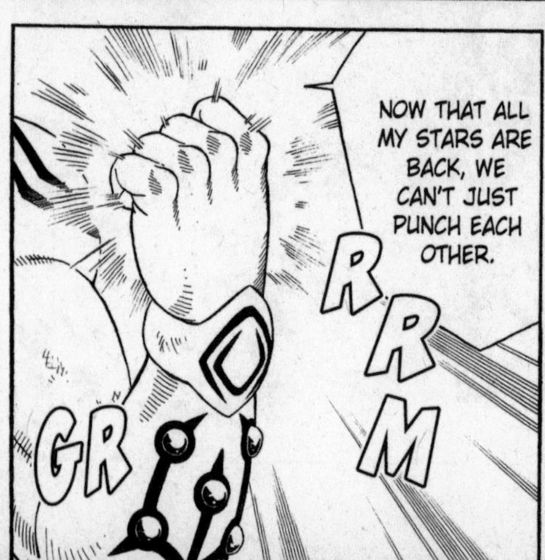
NOW THAT ALL MY STARS ARE BACK, WE CAN'T JUST PUNCH EACH OTHER.
RRRM
GR

READ THIS WAY

THE MOMENT MY DARK POWER FIST TOUCHES YOU, YOUR BODY WILL BE RIPPED APART...
RR
...JUST LIKE YOUR SHIELD-BEARER'S ARMS!
MRR
...

BUT IF THAT'S WHAT YOU WANT, IT CAN'T BE HELPED.

FARE-WELL, ZENON!

GRAAAAH

FAREWELL, LEGENDARY BUSTER, GREATEST ON THE CONTINENT!

!!
SHK
SHK

HFF
HFF
HFF
HFF
HFF
HFF

ARE YOU TRYING TO SHIELD ZENON?
YOU CAN HARDLY MOVE!

GUYS!

READ THIS WAY

OF COURSE!
HFF
THIS TIME, MY WHOLE **BODY** WILL TAKE THE BLOW!
HFF
HFF
EVEN IF WE GET WIPED OUT...
...WE'LL PROTECT ZENON TO THE VERY END!
HFF
WE ARE...
HFF
...ONE!

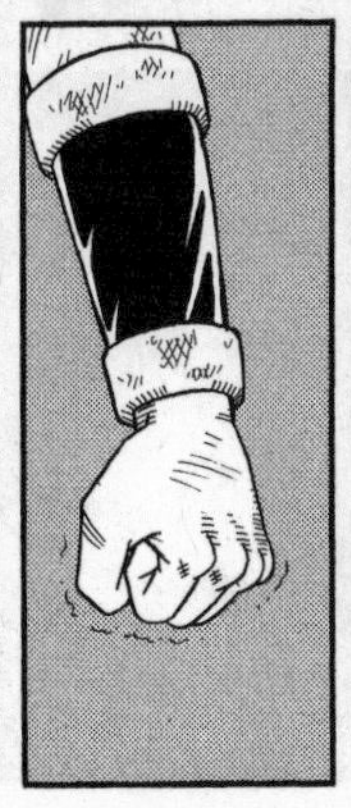

UP TO NOW...
SHF
...WE'VE FOUGHT WITH JUST ONE GOAL.

THANK YOU...
...EVERY-ONE!
WAAAA

BUT WHEN I SAW YOU THROWING YOUR LIVES AWAY FOR BEET...
...I THOUGHT AGAIN...

...THAT WE REALLY ARE...
...BOUND TO EACH OTHER LIKE TRUE BROTHERS!

THE ZENON WARRIORS.

IT WAS A GREAT TEAM!

ZE...

ZENON!

I WILL...
SHK
...BEAT HIM!

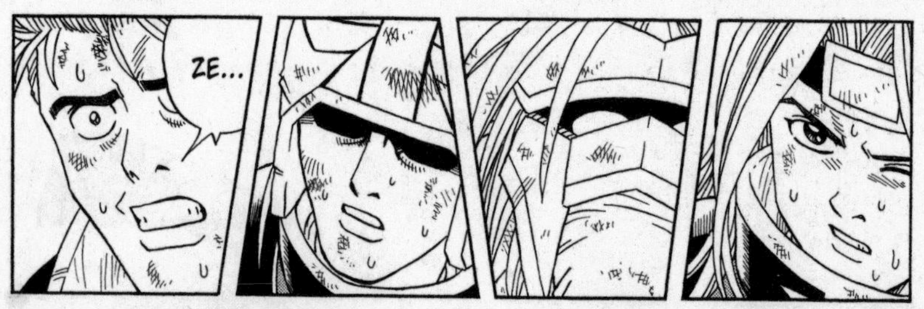
ZE...

DID I HEAR YOU SAY YOU'D BEAT ME?

WAAA

THUK

READ THIS WAY

YEAH.

ZENON!

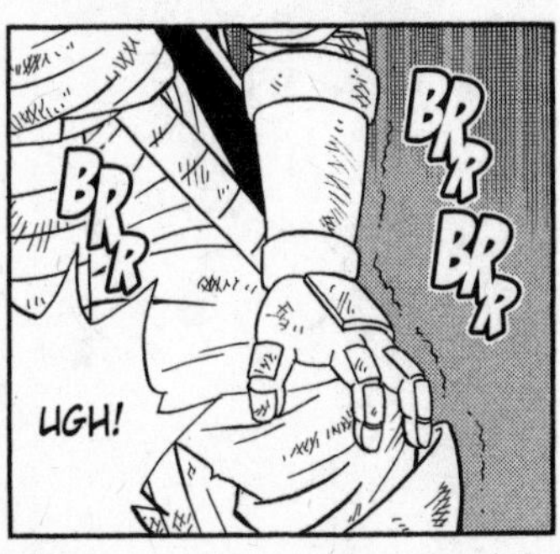
BRRR
BRRR
BRRR
UGH!

SHK

WUMP

NO!
IT'S TOO RECK-LESS!

ZENON!

ZENON!

HEH
NOT A CHANCE.

WHY NOT?
GRP
WHAT IF I HAVE HIDDEN POWER, TOO?

!?

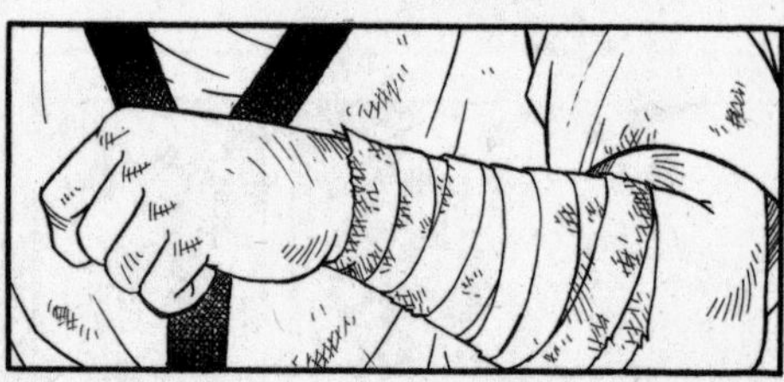

VIP

READ THIS WAY

SHOOF

SHING

B-DMP...

VOOSH

SHOOP

B-DMP
B-DMP

DOOOOM
WHAT THE...
ZENON'S DIVINE POWER!
TH...
THIS GUY...
IT'S GROWING!

VOOM
ARRRRGH
!!!

THUK
DADOOM
ZHAK

GRP
GRR
DOOM
THUK

SZZZZ

THOOM

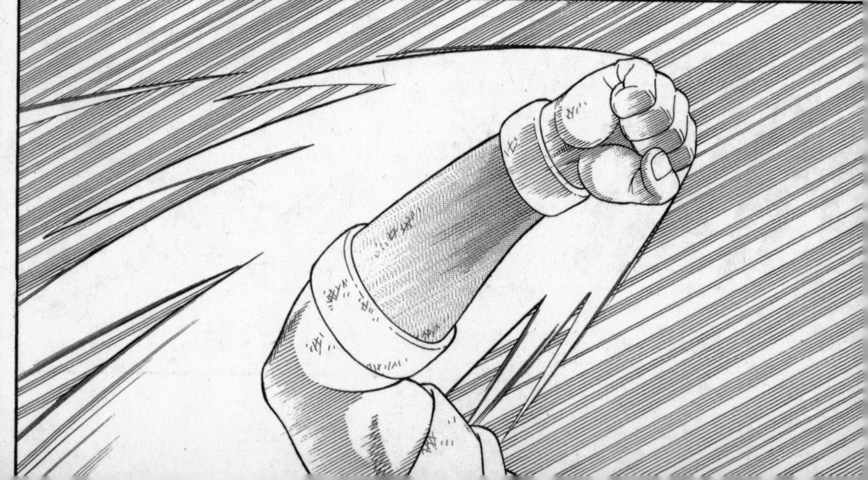

WH
AM

UN-
BELIEVABLE
...
HE THREW
BELTORZE
DOWN WITH
STRENGTH
ALONE!
KABOOOM
DIVINE POWER
IS PULSING OUT
OF HIS BODY...
POWER ON THE
LEVEL OF A FIRST-
CLASS DIVINE
ATTACK!
WHERE
IS IT
COMING
FROM?

READ THIS WAY

THUD
GRRM
GRRM

!!

SO ZENON HAD RESERVE POWER, TOO, HUH?
HEH
PRETTY COCKY!

NO, THAT'S NOT IT!
THAT...
...POWER IS...
VMMM
VMMMM

WHAT THE...
ZENON...
HIS BODY IS...
...FADING...

THAT'S RIGHT.
I'LL VANISH SOON.
IT'S THAT KIND OF POWER.

HUH?
WHAT?
GRRRR

I THINK...
...THIS IS THE POWER TO ADVANCE MY SAIGA TO THE NEXT STEP.

BUT AT MY CURRENT LEVEL, I CAN'T CONTROL IT.
NOW THAT I'VE UNLEASHED IT, IT'S ***CONSUMING*** ME...

KING GRANSISTA TOLD ME NOT TO USE IT, NO MATTER WHAT. HE SEALED IT AWAY...

READ THIS WAY

BUT IF I CAN SAVE MY TEAM-MATES...MY BROTHERS...
...TURNING INTO LIGHT ISN'T SO BAD.
NO... DON'T...
ZENON!
ARRRGH

DON'T!
STOP IT RIGHT NOW!!!

FOOSH

GRRM

GRRRRMR

BELTORZE'S DARK POWER...
...IS INCREASING, TOO!

SNAP
SNAP
SNAP
SNAP

INTERESTING... IT SURE IS HARD TO WITHSTAND.

GRRRRM
SNAP SNAP SNAP SNAP
WHAT A MONSTER!
JUST BY SEEING ZENON DO IT...
GR
SO THIS WAS HOW ...
...TO UNLEASH THE NEXT POWER! THIS WAS WHAT I HAD TO DO!
R
RM
YOU MAKE YOUR POWER MIGHTIER BY BURNING YOUR OWN BODY!
R
MR
NEVER THOUGHT I'D LEARN THAT FROM A *HUMAN*!

DID BELTORZE ALREADY KNOW ABOUT THE POWER BEYOND THE DARK POWER?
THOSE TWO REALLY ARE SPECIAL!
THEY'RE WAY ABOVE ORDINARY PEOPLE AND ORDINARY VANDELS!

GRRRRM

YOU MAY THINK YOU'VE EVENED THE ODDS, BUT THIS ACTUALLY WORKS OUT BETTER FOR ME.
NOW THAT YOU'RE IN THIS STATE, YOU MUST REALIZE...

READ
THIS
WAY

...THAT UNLESS WE CAN CONTROL THIS POWER...
...WE HAVE NO CHOICE BUT TO *BURN OUT!*

THIS IS THE END...
...BEL-TORZE !!

HEH HEH HEH
NO... IT'S THE BEGINNING ...
...ZENON!
...!

IT'S THE ULTIMATE BATTLE...

HA HA HA HA

...I'VE BEEN LOOKING FOR!!

ONLY ONE OF US WILL FALL HERE!
I JUST HAVE TO USE THIS FIGHT TO FIGURE OUT...
...HOW TO HANDLE THIS POWER!

...

KABOOM
I'LL SEIZE IT ALL!
THE POWER AND THE VICTORY!
ONLY YOU...
...WILL VANISH!
ZE...
UGH
ZENON !!
ARGH
DON'T MAKE ME REPEAT MYSELF!

FWASH
I WILL NOT LET YOU LIVE!
MOO

DA
D

THUDDA
THUDDA
SNAP
SNAP
SNAP
SNAP

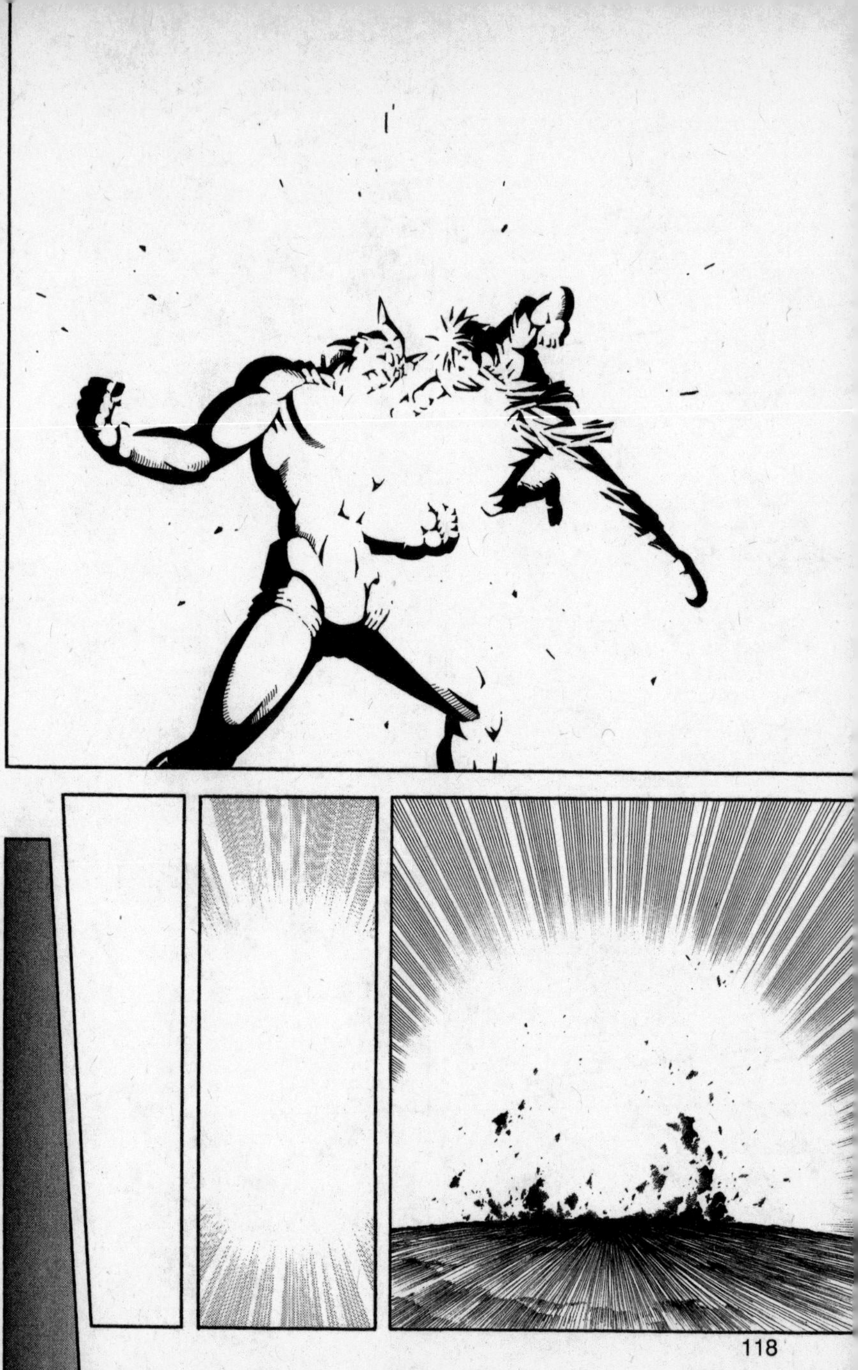

READ THIS WAY

AND...
...THEN WHAT HAP-PENED?

NOTHING. THE FIGHT ENDED THERE.
THERE WAS OUTSIDE INTER-FERENCE.

JUDGING FROM THE STORY ABOUT THE SHIELD-BEARER BEING BLOWN OUT TO BEKATRUTE...
...SOMEONE MUST'VE DROPPED THE ZENON WARRIORS INTO A GAP IN SPACE AND SCATTERED THEM AROUND THE WORLD.

WELL...
...I HAVE A PRETTY GOOD IDEA WHO DID IT, ANYWAY.
SHF

HEH
GRP...
GRRR

THAT MEANS...
...THEY MIGHT **ALL** STILL BE ALIVE!

JUST LIKE YOU WERE BLOWN **HERE**, CRUSS...
...THEY MIGHT BE SPREAD ALL OVER THE WORLD!

THEY MUST HAVE BEEN BADLY INJURED ...
...BUT DON'T WORRY! THEY'RE ALL DEFINITELY ALIVE.

I'M THE SPINDLIEST OF THE FIVE OF US, AND EVEN I SURVIVED!

THERE'S NO CHANCE **ZENON** WAS KILLED!
SHF
HE WAS BEYOND ANYTHING THE REST OF US COULD IMAGINE.

AND YOU'RE ENDOWED WITH THE SAME GIFT.
DON'T FORGET THAT.

YOU CAN MATCH WHAT ZENON DID THAT DAY.
YOU MIGHT EVEN SURPASS HIM!

ME?
SURPASS ZENON?

POALA TOLD ME ABOUT YOUR DREAM!
ENDING THE DARK AGE!
THAT'S GREAT.

NOW THAT YOU'RE ALREADY WALKING THE PATH OF THE BUSTERS, THERE'S NO POINT IN TRYING TO PUSH YOU AWAY LIKE WE USED TO DO.
I'LL DO EVERYTHING IN MY POWER TO HELP YOU REACH THAT DREAM.

CRUSS...

SOB

I PROMISE!
I'M GONNA GET STRONGER!
I'LL DEFEAT VANDELS ALL OVER THE WORLD, ONE AFTER ANOTHER!

AND WHILE I'M AT IT, MAYBE I CAN FIND THE REST OF THE ZENON WARRIORS!
YOU'VE CONVINCED ME, CRUSS!

I'M GONNA DO IT!
STOMP
STOMP

ALL RIGHT!
DAK
GOTTA START THAT SPECIAL TRAINING!

READ THIS WAY

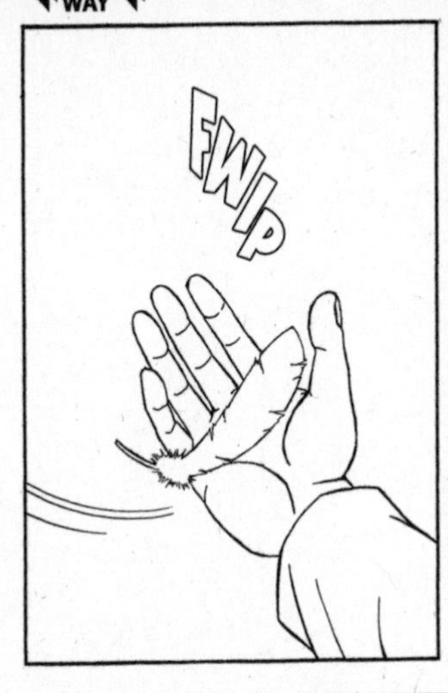
FWIP

IS THAT WHY THOSE BROTHERS ARE REGARDED AS SPECIAL?

WHAT IF ZENON HADN'T GIVEN HIS SAIGA TO BEET? WHAT IF HE HAD UNLEASHED HIS HIDDEN POWER UPON IT?
TAK
THE EXCELLION BLADE MIGHT HAVE EVOLVED INTO SOMETHING INCONCEIV-ABLE!

WHATEVER THE CASE, BEET IS NO LONGER A MERE BUSTER.
HE IS THE EYE OF A HURRICANE THAT WILL ENGULF ALL SEVEN-STAR VANDELS!

READ THIS WAY

BEET
THE VANDEL BUSTER

Chapter 42: Challenge From The Sky!

WHOOOOO
VOOSH
BOOOM
CRASH

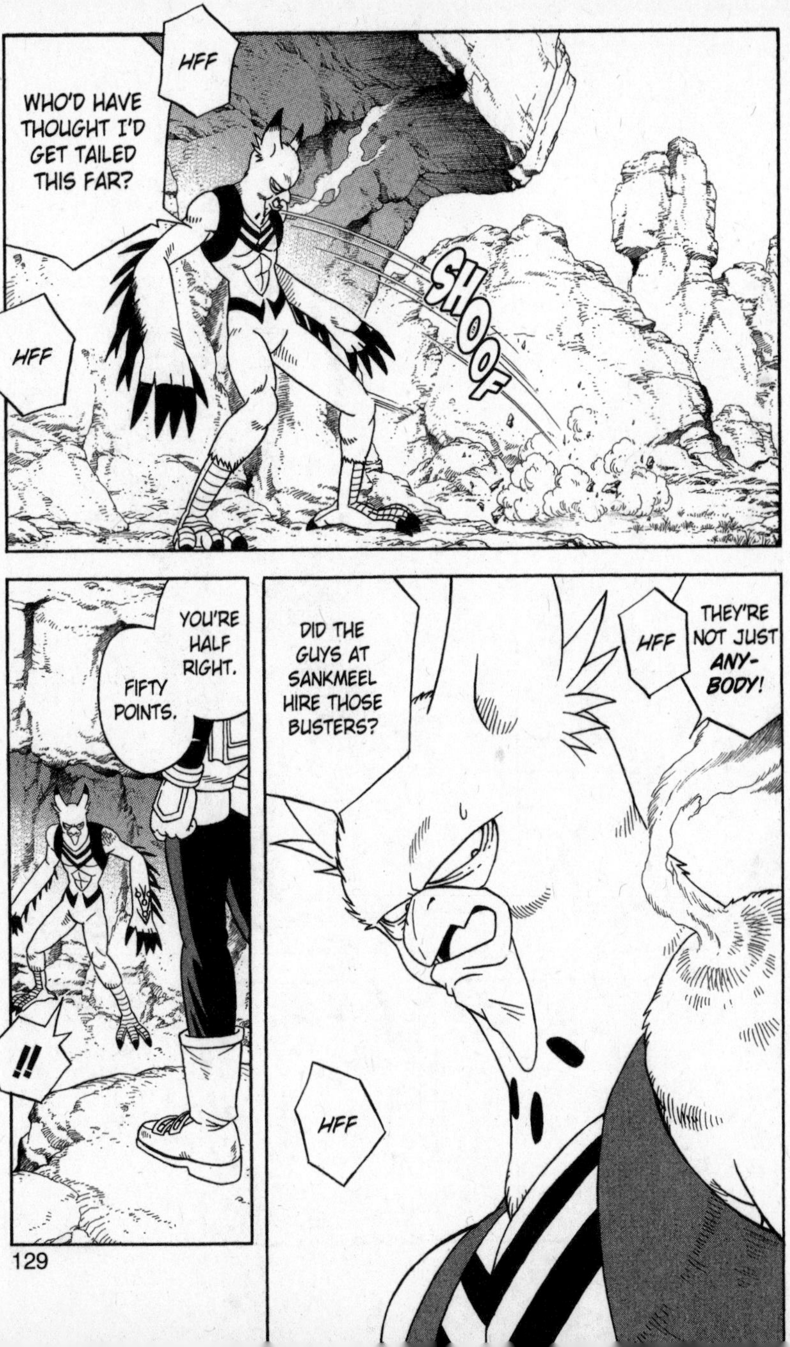

HFF
WHO'D HAVE THOUGHT I'D GET TAILED THIS FAR?
SHOOF
HFF

HFF
THEY'RE NOT JUST ANY-BODY!
DID THE GUYS AT SANKMEEL HIRE THOSE BUSTERS?
HFF

YOU'RE HALF RIGHT.
FIFTY POINTS.
!!

IT'S NOT LIKE WE WERE HIRED.
WE HAPPENED TO BE HERE ON BUSINESS, AND WE HEARD YOU WERE CAUSING TROUBLE.

BUT YOU'RE RIGHT ABOUT US NOT BEING JUST ANYBODY.

HAH...

READ THIS WAY
SHUT YOUR TRAP!
HE'S FAST!
VUSH
VOOM
SHF

BOOOM

!!?

ARRGH
!!

READ THIS WAY
WUP WUP
WOOP
VOOSH
DOOM
SLUK
UGH!

chi
SHF

BAM

VOOM
SLUKKA

THEY'RE ...
...SO STRONG...
BUT WHY?
SPUK
ALL I DID WAS TAKE DOWN 4 OR 5 PLANES...

THAT'S "ALL"?
DO YOU KNOW HOW MANY PEOPLE WERE ON BOARD?
GO MEET THEM IN THE AFTERLIFE!

BOOOOM
ZHAK
RIP
KA-THUD
WHOA!
ARGH !!

BEET!
WE DID IT!
TAKKA
YEAH!
SHF

BUT...
...MY BOOT GOT RIPPED.

WILL YOU BUY ME A NEW PAIR, POALA?

IT'S NOT THAT BAD AT ALL!
WE'LL FIX IT WHEN WE GET BACK.

WHAAAT?
I DON'T GET IT!
YOU BOUGHT ALL NEW GEAR FOR *YOURSELF*!

SHF
WE'RE USING THE MONEY MILFA LOANED US. WE CAN'T WASTE ANY!
AND YOU'VE GOT STRONG SAIGAS. YOU DON'T **NEED** ANY EXTRA GEAR!
...
IT'S TRUE. I ENVY YOU!
HA HA
SHUUUU

IT'S COMMON SENSE. STRENGTHEN THE WEAKER MEMBERS FIRST!
NOOO WAAY!

SANK-MEEL.
A THINLY POPULATED COUNTRY SURROUNDED BY AN IMMENSE EXPANSE OF WILDERNESS.

A FEW PEOPLE MANAGE TO EKE OUT A LIVING IN THIS UNTAMED LAND...

...LIKE SMALL FLOWERS BLOOMING IN THE DESERT.

READ THIS WAY

OVER HERE!
BRING IT QUICKLY!

RRM RRM
YOU'RE FULL OF ENERGY...
...GALA!
OF COURSE I AM!
BEET AND THE OTHERS ARE OUT THERE, GETTING RID OF THE VANDELS IN THE SKY!

IF WE DON'T GET THE PLANE BACK IN TOP CONDITION...
...WE'VE FAILED THEM!

GALA'S TOTALLY LOST HER HEAD OVER THOSE BUSTERS WHO ARRIVED LAST WEEK.
WELL, WE HAVEN'T HAD VISITORS IN AGES.
AND BEET IS SO COOL!
YOU BET!

GUYS! GAB LATER!

BRING IT OVER!

OKAY!

WELCOME BACK!!

BEET!

YO!
YOU'RE WORKING HARD, GALA!

GRAB

READ THIS WAY

THUD

HOW'D IT GO?

SO YOU BEAT ...
...THE VANDEL HARTIS?
YEAH!

ALL RIGHT!

PAPA, DID YOU HEAR?
YOU CAN FLY SAFELY AGAIN!

THAT'S GREAT!

THANK YOU, BEET!

WHAT DO YOU THINK?
THIS ISN'T TOO BAD.
ONCE I FIX IT, YOU CAN STILL WEAR IT. LEAVE IT TO ME!

NOW THAT YOU MENTION IT, WHERE *ARE* THOSE TWO?
THEY'RE AT THE HOUSE.

HA HA
YOU SOUND LIKE POALA.

READ THIS WAY

WE GOT A BIRD MAIL FROM CRUSS.

HE SAYS MILFA SHOULD BE ABLE TO JOIN US SOON.

SO THE NEW GATE'S READY?

SHE SAID SHE'D STICK AROUND UNTIL IT WAS FINISHED. BUT IT LOOKS LIKE SHE'S DONE HER DUTY.
SLADE WENT OFF TO DEAL WITH THE MISSION THAT TOOK HIM TO BEKATRUTE IN THE FIRST PLACE, AND MILFA STAYED BEHIND TO GUARD THE GATE...IT FEELS STRANGE, JUST THE THREE OF US.

IT WAS GOOD THAT WE WENT AHEAD, THOUGH. THAT VANDEL WOULD'VE INTERFERED WITH THE PLANE.
IT WORKED OUT OKAY, HUH?

ONCE MILFA CATCHES UP WITH US ON GUNTRY'S AIRPLANE, WE CAN FINALLY HEAD OUT TO GRANSISTA! THIS COUNTRY HAS A LONG-DISTANCE PLANE THAT CAN HANDLE THE JOURNEY!
YEAH...
AT LONG LAST...

OH, BY THE WAY...

...?
THAT REMINDS ME.

YOU STOPPED THE VANDEL'S ATTACK WITH SOME NEW POWER. IT WASN'T THE DIVINE ATTACK *OR* THE BURST END.
WHAT WAS IT?

OH, THAT?
I DON'T KNOW MYSELF.
IT'S JUST THAT, LATELY, SOMETIMES MY BODY GETS REALLY *HOT*...

...!

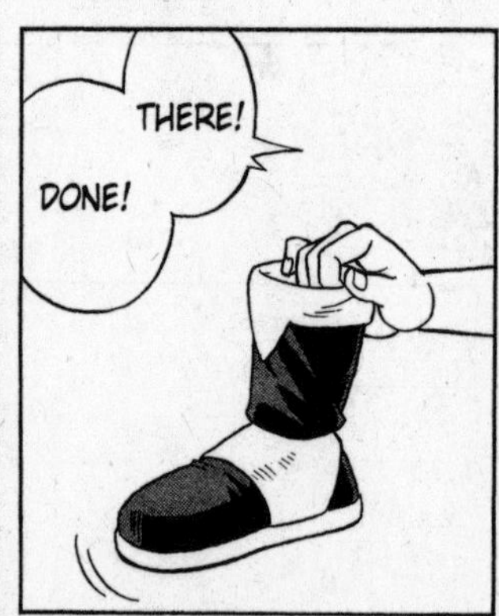
THERE!
DONE!

WOW! YOU'RE AWESOME, GALA!
YOU CAN'T EVEN TELL IT WAS RIPPED!
NO PROB!

READ THIS WAY

THANKS!
YOU SAVED ME!
SHUP

I CAN DO ANYTHING! HOUSEKEEPING, LAUNDRY, SHOE REPAIR, EQUIPPING AIRPLANES...
IF IT'S FOR *YOU*, BEET...
...I'LL DO IT FOREVER!!

...?

HEY, BEET!
MARRY ME!
HUH?
ZOOM

WE'LL HAVE LOTS OF KIDS!
WE'LL MAKE SANKMEEL A JOYFUL PLACE!

I MAY NOT LOOK IT, BUT I'VE GOT *GREAT* FUTURE POTENTIAL!
HA HA...
VA VOOM
MY MOM WAS REALLY HOT, YOU KNOW!

YOU'RE PRETTY SURE OF THINGS...
HMPH.
...HUH?

BESIDES, I'VE GOT POALA.

I'M SORRY ...
...BUT I CAN'T STAY HERE FOREVER.

ARRGH...I'M JEALOUS OF POALA.
SHE'S GOT A STRONG, COMMITTED MAN AS HER FUTURE HUSBAND!
SIGH...
...

GALA!
CHEER UP!
STOMP

YOU VOWED TO SECURE A GOOD MAN WHEN YOU SAW ONE, FOR SANKMEEL'S FUTURE PROSPERITY!
BY FORCE IF NEEDED!
GRIP

READ THIS WAY

YOU'RE RIGHT, PAPA!

I'D BETTER GO AFTER KISSU.
GRP
I THINK HE LIKES ME, YOU KNOW!

JUST WATCH OUT. A GUY LIKE HIM PROBABLY HAS A STRING OF GIRLS.

NO PROBLEM, PAPA! IF I SEE ANY STRANGE WOMEN, I'LL BEAT THEM OFF!
HA!
HO!
SLAP
SLAP
THAT'S THE SPIRIT!

HA
HA
HA
HA
HA
HA
...
THUP
HA
HEH... THEY'RE FUNNY.
THEY SURE ARE... *SPIRITED* IN THESE PARTS...

YEAH.
LET'S WRAP UP FOR THE DAY!

COLBIO, IT'S ABOUT TIME...

THE NIGHT OF...
...THE RED MOON?
ONCE A MONTH, THERE'S A NIGHT WHEN WE'RE FORBIDDEN TO GO OUTSIDE.
ON THAT NIGHT, EVERYONE GOES BEHIND THE BASEMENT GATE AND SITS QUIETLY.

OH YEAH, I FORGOT.
TONIGHT'S THE NIGHT OF THE RED MOON.

READ
THIS
WAY

WHY'S THAT?

DUNNO.

IT'S A CUSTOM THAT STARTED BEFORE I WAS BORN.

THIS IS AN ANCIENT LAND...
...WITH MANY STRANGE CUSTOMS.
PAT
PLEASE RESPECT OUR TRADITIONS.

THINK, PAPA!
NOW THAT BEET AND THE OTHERS HAVE GOTTEN RID OF ALL THE VANDELS...

...WE CAN FLY FREELY TOMORROW AT DAWN!

GO GET POALA AND KISSU, FAST!
OKAY.
I'LL DO THAT.

ALL THE VANDELS, EH?
WELL, IT'S AS GOOD AS THAT.

THERE'S ONE EXCEPTION...
...BUT HE WOULDN'T ATTACK YOUNGSTERS LIKE THEM, EVEN THOUGH THEY SEEM PRETTY TOUGH.

HMPH.
WELL, IF THAT'S THEIR CUSTOM, IT CAN'T BE HELPED.

READ THIS WAY

IT SOUNDS A BIT SUPER-STITIOUS, BUT I GUESS IT'S IMPORTANT TO THEM.

IT'S NOT YOUR DAY OF SLEEP, BUT YOU'D BETTER STAY QUIET, TOO.
YEAH, YEAH.

BUT WHERE'S KISSU GONE OFF TO?
THAT GUY!
HE'S ALWAYS A LITTLE OUT OF STEP...

A SAIGA IS AWAKENING INSIDE POALA.
I'M SURE OF IT.

THAT'S A SAIGA!

I'M SO PATHETIC.

I SHOULD BE HAPPY ABOUT MY TEAMMATE GETTING STRONGER.
INSTEAD, MY FIRST THOUGHT IS OF HOW FAR *I'M* FALLING BEHIND.

SHF

READ THIS WAY

SHF
SHOOF
HUH?

WOOOO

WOOOOO

WHAT IS THIS FEELING?

IT'S COMING ...
...FROM OUTSIDE...

GONG

RRRM

SHOOF

HOOOOY

WHAT'S GOING ON?
SHF
SOME-THING ...
SHF
SHOOF

SOME-THING IS **COMING!**
BRRR

DAKKA
KISSU!

READ THIS WAY

WHY ARE YOU STEPPING OUTSIDE THE GATE?
WE'D BETTER HURRY BACK!

!!

WHAT'S WRONG?
KISSU?
...?

IT'S...IT'S NO GOOD, BEET...
MY BODY... MY LEGS... WON'T MOVE!
GRRR...

WON'T MOVE? WHAT DO YOU...
...

FWIP

BEET...
YEAH!

NOOOO
!!!
URK...

THUK
HUH?
KISSU!

HEY!
WHO ARE YOU?

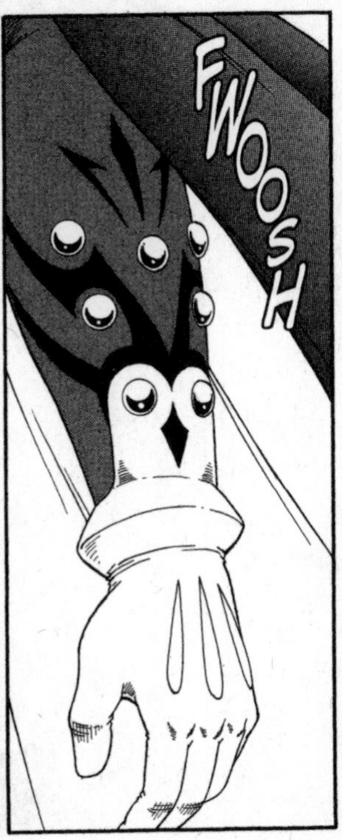
FWOOSH

A VANDEL !!
ANOTHER SEVEN-STAR!

MY NAME IS BARON.
HYOOOO

DID YOU COME TO ATTACK SANKMEEL, TOO?
...
NO.

ALL I'M AFTER IS *BEET*.
ONLY YOU.

!!

I'M NOT INTERESTED IN HUMANS WHO AREN'T WORTH FIGHTING.
YOU DON'T NEED TO WORRY ABOUT THE TOWN.

...

IS HE REALLY A VANDEL?
I CAN'T SENSE ANY BLOOD-LUST IN HIM!

READ THIS WAY

I HAVE A FEELING THIS GUY IS TROUBLE...
BRRR

I BET HE'S MORE DANGEROUS THAN THE ONES WHO COME ON STRONG!

IF YOU'RE NOT IN TOP CONDITION, I DON'T MIND DOING THIS AT ANOTHER TIME AND PLACE...
...BUT FROM THE LOOK OF IT, YOU'RE NOT INJURED...
...AND YOU'RE NOT ALONE.

DO YOU MIND...
...IF WE GET STARTED NOW?

VERY WELL.
SHF...
I'LL GO FIRST!
FWASH

READ THIS WAY

BEET
THE VANDEL BUSTER

Chapter 43: The Frightening Baron!

THUKKA
THUD
WHACK

Chapter 43: The Frightening Baron!

...

UGH...
KOFF...
GRRR

PRETTY GOOD.
HEH

TWITCH

READ
THIS
WAY

I HEAR YOU'RE NOT GOOD AT THE DIVINE ATTACK...

KOFF...
SZZZZ

...BUT YOU CAN AT LEAST SUMMON IT FOR PROTECTION NOW.
YOU KNOW THE BASICS.

IF CRUSS HADN'T TAUGHT ME ABOUT USING THE DIVINE ATTACK FOR DEFENSE...
GRIP
SHUU...
...I'D BE *DEAD* RIGHT NOW.

SHUUUUU

WAAAA

THUK

BRRR BRRR
BRRR

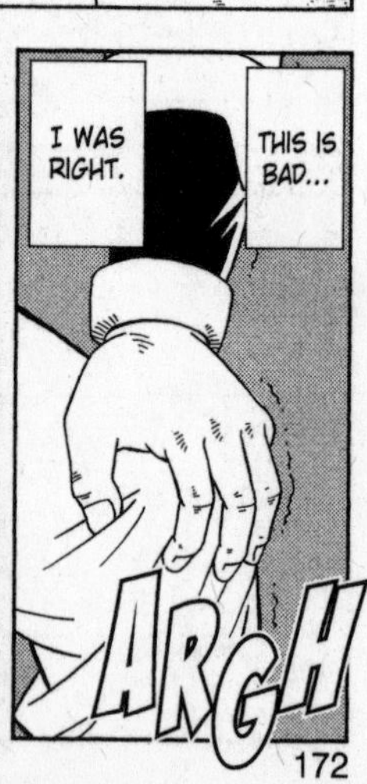
THIS IS BAD...
I WAS RIGHT.
ARGH

WE SHOULDN'T GO UP AGAINST THIS GUY YET!
GRIP

READ THIS WAY

MY FIERCE CELESTIAL PALM IS, IN A WAY, A BAPTIZING BLOW.
I USE IT DETERMINE IF MY OPPONENT HAS THE RIGHT TO FACE ME.

IF HE CAN'T SURVIVE THIS BAPTISM, HE COULDN'T POSSIBLY FIGHT ME, ANYWAY.

IT LOOKS LIKE...
...ONE OF YOU IS *OUT*.

POALA
!!

READ
THIS
WAY

POALAAA
!!!

I HEAR BEET'S VOICE...

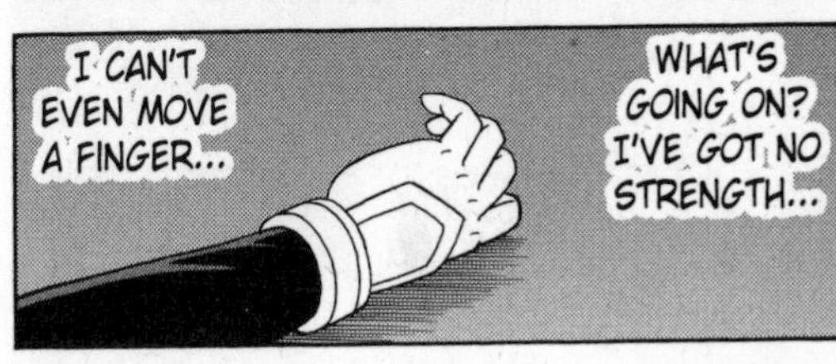
WHAT'S GOING ON? I'VE GOT NO STRENGTH...
I CAN'T EVEN MOVE A FINGER...

I'M IN SERIOUS TROUBLE...
GET UP... GET UP NOW...
...POA... LA...

BAM
KISSU!
HELP POALA!!
BAM

AHH

SHING
SHAAA

MEAN-WHILE...
TAK
...I'LL TAKE ON BARON!!
DADAK
BARON!
SHF

READ THIS WAY

BARON...
BARON!

SO THAT'S...
...WHO HE WAS!

THE LEGENDARY...
...SIR BARON!

SIR BARON?
GLUK GLUK

BUT THE TITLE "SIR" IS...

INDEE

IT'S A *HUMAN* TITLE.

ONCE, THE STRONGEST WARRIOR OF A COUNTRY DUELED WITH BARON. AFTER FIGHTING FIERCELY, HE WAS DEFEATED.

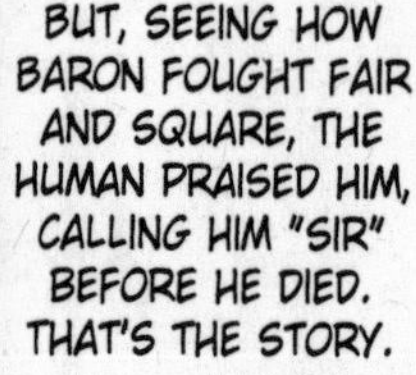
BUT, SEEING HOW BARON FOUGHT FAIR AND SQUARE, THE HUMAN PRAISED HIM, CALLING HIM "SIR" BEFORE HE DIED. THAT'S THE STORY.

OTHER VANDELS THOUGHT IT WAS FUNNY. THEY STARTED USING THE TITLE.

LAUGH-ABLE, ISN'T IT?
A VANDEL RESPEC-TED BY HUMANS.

YES... HEH...

OH, WELL. HE MIGHT BE *ECCENTRIC*, BUT I THINK HE'S AN UNUSUALLY BRIGHT VANDEL... A PEARL AMONG SWINE.

MY HAT GOES OFF TO HIM.

TOK

IF THERE IS A WORD TO DESCRIBE HIM...

...IT'S "EXCEPTIONAL."

YES.

HE'S...

...THE EXCEPTIONAL VANDEL!

BUT HE'S ALSO...

WE CAN'T BEAT HIM!

THERE'S NO WAY!

HE'S ON ANOTHER LEVEL...NOT ONLY ABOVE HUMANS, BUT ABOVE OTHER VANDELS!

THERE'S NOTHING WE CAN DO AGAINST HIM!
THAT'S...

...WHAT MY BODY KNOWS!!

THE MOMENT I SAW HIM...
...I FROZE!

DRAT!

READ THIS WAY

KISSU! WHAT'RE YOU DOING?
HURRY!
POALA IS DYING!
DAK
DAK
DAK
DAK

!!

YES... I'VE GOT TO SAVE MY TEAM-MATES!

OTHER-WISE, BEET AND POALA ARE DOOMED!

DAK
DAK
DAK
DAK

I'VE WORKED SO HARD FOR THIS!

FOR THIS MOMENT!

MOVE!
MOVE, YOU IDIOT!
GRRR

VOOM
TAK

THUK
ARRRRGH
!!!

I MUST FIGHT!
FIGHT!

TOK KA TOK KA
TOK KA

FOR POALA, WHO BELIEVES IN ME!

FOR BEET!!

TOK KA

IF I DON'T FIGHT...
...WHAT ELSE CAN I DO?

THIS... THIS CAN'T BE...
...REAL...
DID I RUN AWAY ?

...

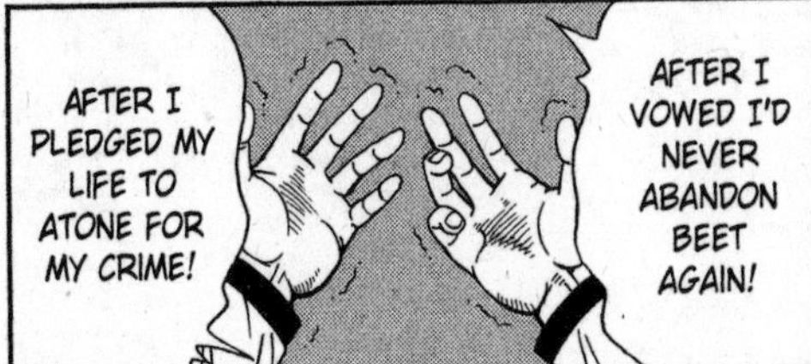
AFTER I VOWED I'D NEVER ABANDON BEET AGAIN!
AFTER I PLEDGED MY LIFE TO ATONE FOR MY CRIME!

I DID TO BEET AND POALA...
...WHAT MY OLD TEAM DID TO ME...

THUD

SLUK
SLUKKA

WELL DONE...
...BEET.

YOU FOUGHT WELL, EVEN THOUGH YOU LOST EVERYTHING.
HFF
HFF

YOUR TEAM-MATES ...
YOUR WEAPONS ...
HFF
HFF

EVEN...
...YOUR FIVE SAIGA.

HFF
HFF
HE'S SO STRONG!
HFF
THEY SAY THERE'S ALWAYS SOMEONE BETTER THAN THE BEST...BUT HE'S OUT OF THIS WORLD!
HFF
BUT EVEN SO...
...IT CAN'T END THIS WAY...

GRP
THUMP

I WON'T LET IT HAPPEN!
GRRK
IT CAN'T END LIKE THIS!
GRRRK

INDOMITABLE, INDEED!
I REGRET HAVING TO KILL HIM JUST LIKE THAT...

READ THIS WAY

LET'S CALL IT QUITS.

TODAY, FOR THE SAKE OF YOUR FIGHTING SPIRIT...

YOU'LL LET HIM OFF THE HOOK?
I DON'T THINK SO, SIR!

HYSTARIO!

AN... ANOTHER... VANDEL?

ZHK

READ THIS WAY

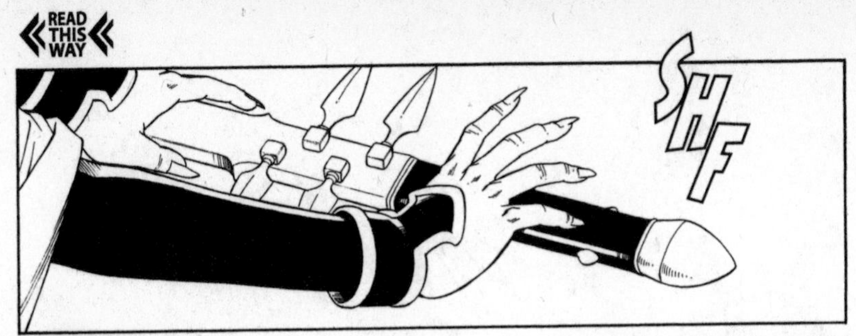
SHF

TWAAA
GN

AGAIN?
ENOUGH OF THAT...
SHOOOF

THOOM

LAST TIME, I NOTED YOUR MOVEMENTS.

NOW...
...THE GAME CHANGES PLAYERS!

BEET
THE VANDEL BUSTER

BEET THE WORLD

THE WORLD OF *BEET, King of Adventure* • PART 6

Beet's desperate battle against the seven-star Vandels is getting even more intense! The excitement is deepening! In Part 6 of our special section, we'll close in on the secrets of the world of Beet.

REGULAR WEAPONS

GRP

WARRIORS' BASIC EQUIPMENT! COLORFUL VARIATIONS!

The weapons Busters use in battle are commonly called "regular weapons." The Saiga aren't considered regular weapons by most Busters. The most effective and cheapest way to get regular weapons is to buy them. Since it's the Age of Darkness, even ordinary citizens carry weapons, and every town has a weapon store. New Busters generally start with used weapons in their first battles and polish their skills. These weapons are adequate up to about Level 10.

As Busters become stronger and better trained, they begin making and using custom weapons, which they can order through an Appraiser's House. Naturally, these customized weapons are much more expensive than the ones sold at regular weapon stores. As a Buster learns which weapons are best suited to his or her fighting style, he or she determines the form of the Saiga, the Buster's ideal weapon. In that respect, using regular weapons is crucial to each Buster's future.

▲ The Zenon Warriors' Saigas were based on their regular weapons.

Guns

Guns are powerful but expensive. Nonetheless, a gun is the perfect weapon to support the team from a distance. Every Buster team should have at least one marksman.

TAKKA TAKKA TAKKA

▲ This is Poala's weapon, the Arm Gun.

BA
NG

▲ This is a handgun used by the Winged Knight. Guns are usually carried as a backup weapon. A Buster who specializes in guns is rare.

Swords & Spears

Swords and spears are the most commonly used weapons. Because there are many varieties, it's easy to find one that suits a Buster.

▲ This is Slade's regular weapon. It's a halberd-style spear called Grave.

THUK

▶ It seems like Beet makes his own spear every time he fights.

▲ This is a popular longsword used by Glest.

Special Equipment

There are many weapons specially designed for Busters. Among them are small weapons that amplify Divine Power.

▶▼ Kissu's Blast Circle, when amplified by Divine Power, turns into a giant circle of light.

SHF
SHF
SLAP
BA

◀ These are Milfa's Silver Cuffs.

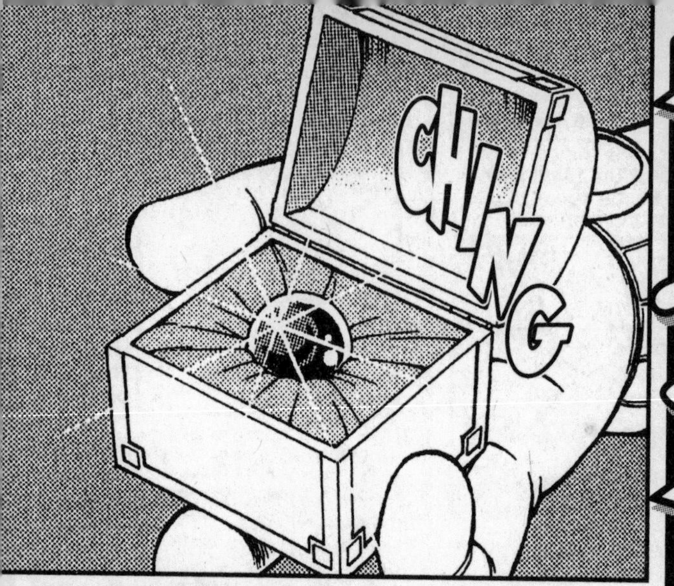
CHING

STARS

The greatest honor Vandels seek is the "star." The number of stars determines a Vandel's status. Although there are exceptions, most Vandels fight desperately to gain stars.
The suffering they inflict upon the human world is acknowledged as a great achievement. When a Vandel creates a certain level of damage, he or she is granted a star. It's similar to the Levels awarded to Busters. Just as people try to raise their fighting spirit against Vandels by increasing Busters' Levels and giving them money, Vandels use stars and Sorcery Bills to stir up their desire to attack humans. Vandels are born with one star, then get promoted to two-star, three-star and so forth.

Eight stars represent the highest status. Apparently, the first Vandel to win eight stars will rule the other Vandels and the world.
But what power does the eight-star Vandel gain? Have any Vandels ever won eight stars? These are unanswered questions. What will happen when one of the current seven-star Vandels wins another star?

▲ The stars that shine on the left arms of Vandels are proof of honor.

THEY ARE THE PROOF OF EVIL DEEDS! WHAT WILL HAPPEN WHEN EIGHT STARS SHINE?

SHAAA
HOW IS IT?
DO I LOOK GOOD?
TADAH

▼ A star being wedged onto a Vandel's arm.

▲◀ Receiving a star from Shagie is a blissful moment for a Vandel.

GRANTING OF A STAR

Holding the battle records of every Vandel in his hand, Shagie is the only Vandel who has the right to grant a star. He uses Dark Power to wedge a star, which rests inside a small box, onto a Vandel's left arm. Naturally, the larger the number of the stars, the more destruction a Vandel has to create to win the next star. The difference between seven stars and eight stars is especially vast.

SWALLOWING THE STAR

▼ Once the first star is charged with Dark Power, it's pushed into the body and sealed.

"Swallowing the Star" is a training method that takes advantage of the star's ability to accumulate Dark Power. It is a risky method that can only be used by high-level Vandels with overwhelming power.

DEMISE

When a Vandel dies, the stars in his or her arm break into pieces. Because of this, no Vandel can kill another and steal stars from the victim. Apparently, Vandels are biologically programmed this way. Similarly, when a star is ripped off a Vandel, its color darkens and it loses its luster.

SNAP
SNIPSNAP

▲◀ Stars are breaking into pieces, one after the other. This is the demise of a powerful Vandel.

THE EYES of DARKNESS

THE CREATORS OF THE VANDELS! THE LORDS OF DARKNESS, SHROUDED IN MYSTERY!

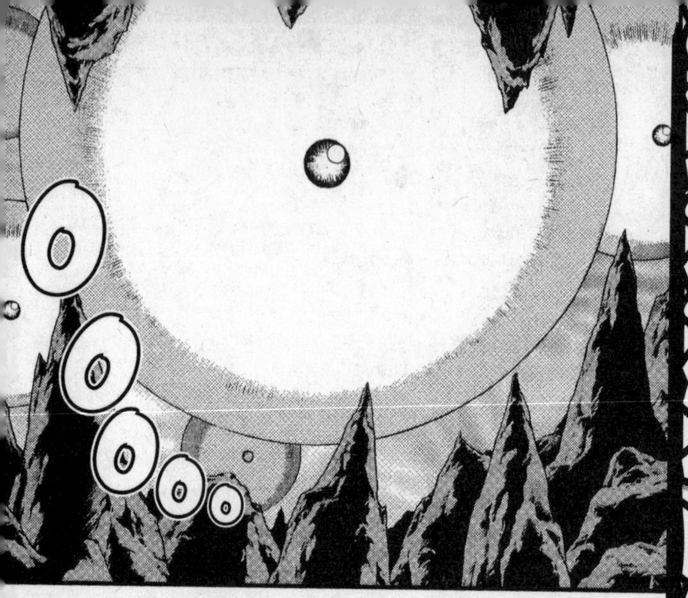

These are giant eyes that float in the scorching heat of lava, deep under the basement of the Dark House of Sorcery. They are none other than the creators of the Vandels. The world of Vandels is full of mysteries, but the Eyes of Darkness are, without doubt, the greatest mystery of all. From the information provided so far, it's clear that Vandels are born in their adult form. Unlike other living things, Vandels do not breed, and no two Vandels are the same. If the Eyes of Darkness gave birth to such strange creatures, their mystery must be the mystery of the Vandels' birth itself. Indeed, it isn't an exaggeration to say that they are at the root of the Age of Darkness!

▲ Shagie, the Chief of the House, is the messenger of the Eyes of Darkness.

As the parents of all Vandels, they rule as omnipotent beings... If Beet is to end the Age of Darkness, he cannot avoid this enemy. Currently, it appears that Shagie is the only Vandel who is allowed audience with the Eyes of Darkness. Let's hope the day will come when Beet can face them directly.

CLOSING IN ON THE MYSTERY OF THE EYES OF DARKNESS!!

THE EYES OF DARKNESS!

THEIR LOCATION

Shagie descends from the lowest floor of the basement of the Dark House of Sorcery, using a special elevator, to visit the Eyes of Darkness. The Dark House of Sorcery itself is located at the so-called spring of sorcery on the border of the magical world. It is not known how deep its deepest spot is, but it's clear that much lies beneath the surface.

RUMBLE

▲▶◀ Shagie is the only one who can use the elevator. It's in a strictly forbidden area.

THEIR NATURE

YES. I'M LOOKING FORWARD TO IT!
WHO WILL BECOME THE FIRST EIGHT-STAR VANDEL, PUSHING ASIDE ALL OTHER VANDELS?

▲It appears that Shagie alone can hear the groan of the Eyes as some language...

What are the Eyes of Darkness? A big mystery is whether they actually exist. If what we've seen is their true form, either each of them is a single giant eye, or they're all the eyes of an even more gigantic creature. If the latter is true, what kind of creature could it be? There's also the possibility that the eyes are only illusions or projections from somewhere else. If that's the case, what are their true forms and whereabouts? When will the answers come to light?

THEIR OBJECTIVE

Their goals, at least, seem clear. The primary objective of the Eyes of Darkness is to produce a Vandel strong enough to win eight stars. Using Beet as a target, they've driven the seven-star Vandels to battle. But once the eight-star Vandel arises, what do they want him to do? Expand their territory? Exterminate humanity? Or something else? Beet's upcoming battles may show us the answer!

▲◀ Who is the Vandel sought by the Eyes of Darkness?

Coming Next Volume...

Separated from his teammates, Beet realizes that he's up against his toughest adversary yet…and when Sir Baron removes his helmet and reveals his bizarre secret, things only get worse! Against a Vandel this powerful, even the Winged Knight seems to have met his match. But when Sir Baron turns upon the innocent villagers of Sankmeel, one warrior finally decides to take a stand. At long last, Kissu is ready to fight to the limit!

Coming in October 2007!

SHONEN JUMP
BEET THE VANDEL BUSTER
BEET
THE VANDEL BUSTER
Now
Available
on DVD
DO YOU HAVE A SAIGA
HIDDEN IN YOUR HEART

テニスの王子様
THE PRINCE OF TENNIS™
SJ
Action! Intrigue! Espionage! High School tennis has never been this exciting!
ALL BOOKS $7.99! AND UNDER
SJ PRINCE OF TENNIS 1 Takeshi Konomi
THE PRINCE OF TENNIS
SHONEN JUMP GRAPHIC NOVEL
Story & Art by
Takeshi Konomi
volume 1
Manga on sale now!

WHISTLE!™
Manga on sale now!
WHISTLE!
SHONEN JUMP GRAPHIC NOVEL
Daisuke Higuchi
volume 1
When the whistle blows, get ready for rip-roaring soccer action!
SHONEN JUMP

SUBSCRIBE TODAY & BECOME A MEMBER OF THE SHONEN JUMP SUBSCRIBER CLUB...
You'll get:
*Access to Exclusive Online Content!
*50% Savings Off the Newsstand Price!
*Exclusive Premiums!
All this available ONLY to Subscribers!
SHONEN JUMP
THE WORLD'S MOST POPULAR MANGA
FILL OUT THE SUBSCRIPTION CARD ON THE OTHER SIDE, OR SUBSCRIBE ONLINE AT:
www.shonenjump.com